ABOUT THE AU'

Anthony Robbins has devoted more than half his life to helping people discover and develop their own unique qualities of greatness. Considered the nation's leader in the science of peak performance, he is the founder and chairman of the Anthony Robbins Companies, which are committed to assisting people in achieving personal and professional mastery.

Robbins has served as a peak performance consultant for the executives of such organisations as IBM, AT&T, American Express and the United States Army as well as professional sports teams such as the Los Angeles Dodgers, the America's Cup team and gold medal-winning Olympic athletes. Robbins also provides ongoing coaching and consulting to a number of prominent world figures and is the primary adviser in the re-engineering efforts of several organisations and even communities.

Robbins' special passion is to make the world a better place to live by assisting individuals in captaining their destinies – whether that means fostering their relationships with their families, directing their focus to achieve their goals, relieving emotional or financial distress, or making profound contributions to their communities and country. Throughout the years he has unselfishly given his energy and resources to those in need and in 1991 he formed a non-profit foundation to aid underprivileged children, homeless individuals, senior citizens and the prison population.

Mr Robbins lives in California with his wife and children.

Tony's message comes straight from the heart: by doing simple acts of kindness for others, we can't help but lift ourselves up, too'

Ted Danson

'Tony Robbins inspired me to take my career to the next level. Having attended all of his live courses, he definitely is the number one communicator in the world. He really knows how to bring out the best in you so that you consistently peak perform'

Roger Black, World Olympic medallist,
BBC television presenter and motivational speaker